Everything You Wanted to Know About

...But Forgot You Wanted to Ask

Every effort has been made in preparing this book to provide accurate and up-to-date information that is in accord with accepted standards and practice at the time of publication Nevertheless, the author, editors, and publisher can make no warranties that the information contained herein is totally free from error, not least because clinical standards are constantly changing through research and regulation. The authors, editors, and publisher therefore disclaim all liability for direct or consequential damages resulting from the use of material contained in this book. Readers are strongly advised to pay careful attention to information provided by the manufacturer of any drugs or equipment that they plan to use.

PUBLISHED BY NEI PRESS, an imprint of NEUROSCIENCE EDUCATION INSTITUTE
Carlsbad, California, United States of America

NEUROSCIENCE EDUCATION INSTITUTE
1930 Palomar Point Way, Suite 101
Carlsbad, California 92008

http://www.neiglobal.com

Printed in the United States of America
First Edition, October 2008

Typeset in Myriad Pro

Library of Congress Cataloging-in-Publication Data
ISBN 1-4225-0033-0

Table of Contents

Table of Contents (cont'd)

CME Information

Overview

Even though attention deficit hyperactivity disorder (ADHD) was once considered a childhood disorder, it has become clear that it also affects a significant number of adults. As the symptoms of ADHD change throughout the life of a patient, it is important to optimize treatment strategies. Additionally, adults with ADHD often have comorbid disorders which may take center stage and delay the correct diagnosis of ADHD. It is therefore imperative to rule out comorbid disorders and to take them into account when considering the appropriate treatment plan. In this booklet, we examine the neurobiology of ADHD, the presentation of it across the ages, the type of disorders comorbid with ADHD, and finally, the different treatment options available.

Target Audience

This CME activity has been developed for MDs specializing in psychiatry. There are no prerequisites for this activity. Physicians in all specialties who are interested in psychopharmacology, as well as nurses, psychologists, and pharmacists, are welcome for advanced study.

Statement of Need

The following unmet needs regarding ADHD were revealed following a vigorous assessment of activity feedback, expert faculty assessment, literature review, and through new medical knowledge:

- the majority of studies on ADHD have been carried out in children but it is now being recognized that problems can not only continue through adolescence and into adulthood but may not be diagnosed until this time
- although there are a number of rating scales to aid diagnosis and tracking of symptoms of ADHD, they may not be used as often as they should be; additionally, diagnosis of adult ADHD needs a separate set of rating scales which reflect the differences in symptoms compared to childhood ADHD
- a large proportion of patients with ADHD also have comorbid illnesses, which can have an important impact on treatment selection
- there are a number of new formulations of current ADHD medications that are being tested and integrated into the market; these may help improve adherence but this factor can be greatly enhanced by patient education and therapy

To help fill these unmeet needs, quality improvement efforts need to

- illuminate participants on the ways ADHD can continue into adolescence and adulthood and the problems that can continue to occur in people with this disorder
- inform participants on the different rating scales that can be used for both childhood and adulthood ADHD and how cognitive testing can enhance diagnosis
- educate the participants on how to recognize and treat comorbid illnesses in patients with ADHD
- inform participants about novel formulations of current and future ADHD medications and discuss the role of therapy in ADHD and how it can enhance adherence

CME Information (cont'd)

Learning Objectives

After completing this activity, participants should be better able to:

- recognize how ADHD symptoms change as a patient grows up and how previously unrecognized ADHD can manifest in an adult
- use measurement tools to track a patient's symptoms
- better assess comorbid illness in adult ADHD patients in order to maximize treatment
- integrate new treatment formulations and therapy into current practice

Accreditation and Credit Designation Statements

The Neuroscience Education Institute is accredited by the Accreditation Council for Continuing Medical Education to provide continuing medical education for physicians.

The Neuroscience Education Institute designates this educational activity for a maximum of 2.5 *AMA PRA Category 1 Credits*™. Physicians should only claim credit commensurate with the extent of their participation in the activity. Non-physicians may receive a certificate of participation for completing this activity.

Activity Instructions

This CME activity is in the form of a printed monograph and incorporates instructional design to enhance your retention of the information and pharmacological concepts that are being presented. You are advised to go through the figures in this activity from beginning to end, followed by the text, and then complete the posttest and activity evaluation. The estimated time for completion of this activity is 2.5 hours.

Instructions for CME Credit

To receive your certificate of CME credit or participation, please complete the posttest (you must score at least 70% to receive credit) and activity evaluation found at the end of the monograph and mail or fax them to the address/number provided. Once received, your posttest will be graded and a certificate sent if a score of 70% or more was attained. **Alternatively, you may complete the posttest and activity evaluation online and immediately print your certificate.** There is no fee for this activity.

NEI Disclosure Policy

It is the policy of the Neuroscience Education Institute to ensure balance, independence, objectivity, and scientific rigor in all its educational activities. Therefore, all individuals in a position to influence or control content development are required by NEI to disclose any financial relationships or apparent conflicts of interest that may have a direct bearing on the subject matter of the activity. Although potential conflicts of interest are identified and resolved prior to the activity being presented, it remains for the participant to determine whether outside interests reflect a possible bias in either the exposition or the conclusions presented.

These materials have been peer-reviewed to ensure the scientific accuracy and medical relevance of information presented and its independence from commercial bias. The Neuroscience Education Institute takes responsibility for the content, quality, and scientific integrity of this CME activity.

CME Information (cont'd)

Individual Disclosure Statements

Author/Developer

Laurence Mignon, PhD
Senior Medical Writer, Neuroscience Education Institute, Carlsbad, CA
Stockholder: Aspreva Pharmaceuticals Corporation; Vanda Pharmaceuticals Inc.; ViroPharma Incorporated

Content Editors

Meghan Grady
Director, Content Development, Neuroscience Education Institute, Carlsbad, CA
No other financial relationships to disclose.

Stephen M. Stahl, MD, PhD
Adjunct Professor, Department of Psychiatry, University of California, San Diego School of Medicine, San Diego, CA
Board Member: Cypress; NovaDel; Tetragenix
Grant/Research: AstraZeneca; Biovail; Bristol-Myers Squibb; Cephalon; Cyberonics; Eli Lilly; Forest; GlaxoSmithKline; Janssen; Neurocrine; Organon; Pamlab; Pfizer; Sepracor; Shire; Somaxon; Wyeth
Consultant/Advisor: ACADIA; Amylin; Asahi Kasei; AstraZeneca; Avera; Azur; BioLaunch; Biovail; Bionevia; Boehringer Ingelheim; Bristol-Myers Squibb; Cephalon; CSC; Cyberonics; Cypress; Endo; Eli Lilly; EPIX; Fabre-Kramer; Forest; GlaxoSmithKline; Jazz; Labopharm; Lundbeck; Marinus; Neurocrine; NeuroMolecular; Neuronetics; NovaDel; Novartis; Noven; Nuvis; Organon; Otsuka; Pamlab; Pfizer; Pierre Fabre; Sanofi-Synthélabo; Schering-Plough; Sepracor; Servier; Shire; SK; Solvay; Somaxon; Takeda; Tetragenix; Vanda; Wyeth
Speakers Bureau: Pfizer; Wyeth

Peer Reviewer

Meera Narasimhan, MD
Professor, Department of Psychiatry; Director of Biological Research, Office of Biological Research, Department of Neuropsychiatry and Behavioral Science, University of South Carolina School of Medicine, Columbia, SC
Grant/Research: AstraZeneca Pharmaceuticals LP; Bristol-Myers Squibb Company; Forest Laboratories, Inc.; Janssen, L.P.
Consultant/Advisor: Bristol-Myers Squibb Company; Eli Lilly and Company
Speakers Bureau: AstraZeneca Pharmaceuticals LP; Bristol-Myers Squibb Company; Eli Lilly and Company

Editorial & Design Staff

Tory Daley, MPH
Program Development Manager, Neuroscience Education Institute, Carlsbad, CA
No other financial relationships to disclose.

Stacey L. Hughes
Vice President, Program Development, Neuroscience Education Institute, Carlsbad, CA
No other financial relationships to disclose.

CME Information (cont'd)

Nancy Muntner
Director, Medical Illustrations, Neuroscience Education Institute, Carlsbad, CA
No other financial relationships to disclose.

Disclosed financial relationships have been reviewed by the Neuroscience Education Institute CME Advisory Board to resolve any potential conflicts of interest. All faculty and planning committee members have attested that their financial relationships do not affect their ability to present well-balanced, evidence-based content for this activity.

Disclosure of Off-Label Use
This educational activity may include discussion of unlabeled and/or investigational uses of agents that are not approved by the FDA. Please consult the product prescribing information for full disclosure of labeled uses.

Disclaimer
The information presented in this educational activity is not meant to define a standard of care, nor is it intended to dictate an exclusive course of patient management. Any procedures, medications, or other courses of diagnosis or treatment discussed or suggested in this educational activity should not be used by clinicians without full evaluation of their patients' conditions and possible contraindications or dangers in use, review of any applicable manufacturer's product information, and comparison with recommendations of other authorities. Primary references and full prescribing information should be consulted.

Participants have an implied responsibility to use the newly acquired information from this activity to enhance patient outcomes and their own professional development. The participant should use his/her clinical judgment, knowledge, experience, and diagnostic decision-making before applying any information, whether provided here or by others, for any professional use.

Grant Information
This activity is supported by an educational grant from Shire Pharmaceuticals Inc.

Chapter 1:

Neurobiology, Circuits and Genetics

Objectives:

- Define cortical-striatal-thalamic-cortical (CSTC) loops
- Explain the symptoms of ADHD and how they relate to specific CSTC loops
- Describe the importance of executive function and arousal in ADHD
- Identify methods used to test for executive function
- Understand the genetics of ADHD

Deconstructing the Syndrome into DSM-IV Diagnostic Symptoms

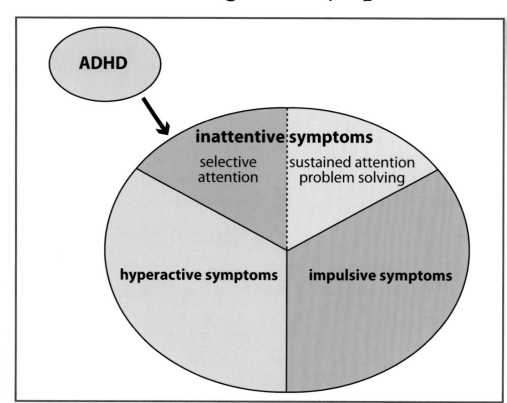

FIGURE 1.1. Attention deficit hyperactivity disorder (ADHD) has been divided into three clusters of symptoms: hyperactive, impulsive, and inattentive. As each patient presents with a specific degree of impairment in these three categories, a patient can, according to the Diagnostic and Statistical Manual of Mental Disorders IV (DSM-IV), be placed into the following subtypes: the predominantly inattentive type, the predominantly hyperactive-impulsive type and lastly the combined type, which is also the most frequent one.

Important Brain Areas in Executive Function and Motor Control

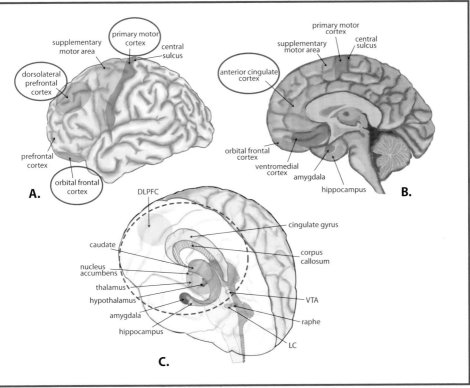

DLPFC: dorsolateral prefrontal cortex; LC: locus coeruleus; VTA: ventral tegmental area

FIGURE 1.2. To better understand the underlying pathophysiology of ADHD, it is important to know which brain circuits are affected and how they can impact other processes. Four different brain regions (red circles in A and B) are hypothesized to be affected in ADHD, and may lead to altered functioning of their respective cortical-striatal-thalamic-cortical (CSTC) loops (dotted red circle in C, and Fig. 1.4.).

How are Core Symptoms of ADHD Linked to a Malfunctioning Prefrontal Cortex?

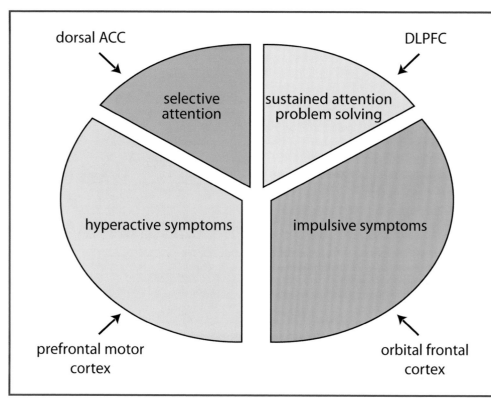

ACC: anterior cingulate cortex; DLPFC: dorsolateral prefrontal cortex

FIGURE 1.3. Inefficient information processing in the brain areas listed in Fig. 1.2. can hypothetically lead to the different symptoms of ADHD and other psychiatric disorders: malfunctioning of the dorsal ACC results in problems with selective attention; malfunctioning of the DPLFC results in problems with sustained attention; impairments in the prefrontal motor cortex lead to symptoms of hyperactivity; impairments in the orbital frontal cortex lead to impulsive symptoms. These brain areas are part of a circuitry referred to as the cortical-striatal-thalamic-cortical loops, which are further explained in Fig. 1.4.

Hypothetical Malfunctioning CSTC Loops in ADHD

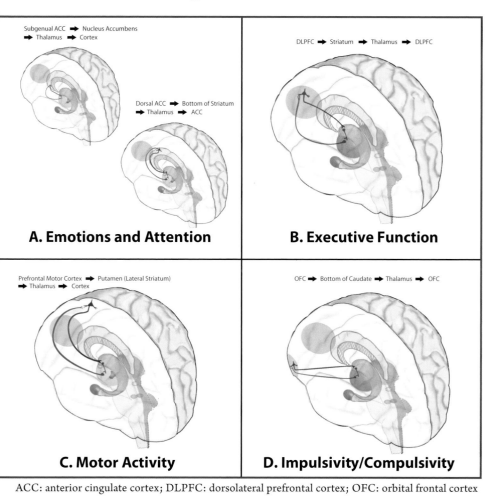

Subgenual ACC ➡ Nucleus Accumbens ➡ Thalamus ➡ Cortex

Dorsal ACC ➡ Bottom of Striatum ➡ Thalamus ➡ ACC

A. Emotions and Attention

DLPFC ➡ Striatum ➡ Thalamus ➡ DLPFC

B. Executive Function

Prefrontal Motor Cortex ➡ Putamen (Lateral Striatum) ➡ Thalamus ➡ Cortex

C. Motor Activity

OFC ➡ Bottom of Caudate ➡ Thalamus ➡ OFC

D. Impulsivity/Compulsivity

ACC: anterior cingulate cortex; DLPFC: dorsolateral prefrontal cortex; OFC: orbital frontal cortex

FIGURE 1.4. (A) Emotions and attention are hypothetically regulated by the subgenual ACC–nucleus accumbens–thalamus loop and the dorsal ACC–bottom of striatum–thalamus loop, respectively. (B) Executive function is hypothetically regulated by the DLPFC–striatum–thalamus loop, and (C) the prefrontal motor cortex–lateral striatum–thalamus loop hypothetically regulates motor activity. (D) Impulsivity and compulsivity are hypothetically regulated by the OFC–bottom of striatum–thalamus loop.

Assessing Sustained Attention and Problem Solving with the N-Back Test

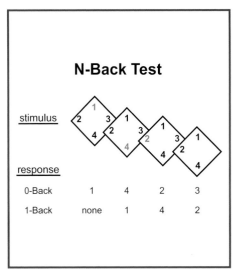

N-Back Test

stimulus				
response				
0-Back	1	4	2	3
1-Back	none	1	4	2

n-back test

inattentive

overactivation
normal
baseline
hypoactivation

FIGURE 1.5. The N-Back test is used to assess executive function, especially sustained attention. In the 0-back variant, a participant looks at a number on the screen, and presses a button to indicate which number it is. In the 1-back variant, a participant only looks at the first number; when the second number appears the participant is supposed to press a button corresponding to the first number. Higher "N" numbers are correlated with increased difficulty in the test.

FIGURE 1.6. The level of activation of the dor solateral prefrontal cortex (purple circle) can be assessed using the N-back test. As shown in Fig. 1.4.B, executive function, especially sustained attention, is hypothetically associated with the following CSTC loop: DLPFC–striatum–thalamus. Inefficient information processing within this loop would thus cause a person to lack sustained attention on a task and have problems with organization, follow through and problem solving.

Assessing Selective Attention with the Stroop Task

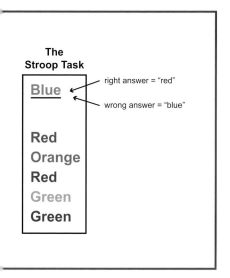

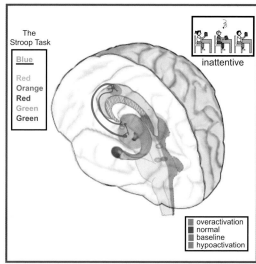

FIGURE 1.7. The Stroop task is used to assess selective attention, and requires the participants to name the color with which a word is written, instead of saying the word itself. In the present case, for example, the word "blue" is written in red. The correct answer is therefore "red," while "blue" is the incorrect choice.

FIGURE 1.8. The level of activation of the anterior cingulate cortex (purple circle) can be determined using the Stroop task. As shown in Fig. 1.4.A, selective attention is hypothetically associated with the ACC–striatum–thalamus CSTC loop. Inefficient information processing within this loop would thus cause a person to pay little attention to detail, make careless mistakes, not listen, be distracted and lose valuables.

Impulsivity is Modulated by the Orbital Frontal Cortex

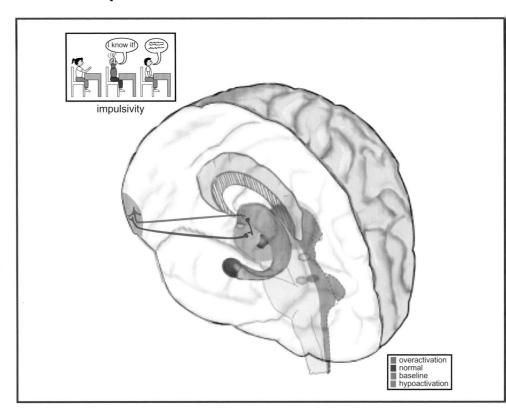

FIGURE 1.9. As shown in Fig. 1.4.D, impulsivity is hypothetically associated with the orbital frontal cortex (purple circle)–bottom of striatum–thalamus CSTC loop. Inefficient modulation within this loop would thus cause a person to talk excessively, blurt things out, not wait in line, and interrupt others.

Motor Hyperactivity Is Modulated by the Prefrontal Motor Cortex

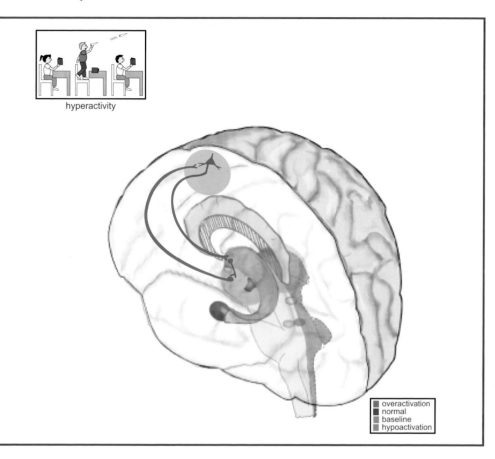

FIGURE 1.10. Motor hyperactivity is hypothetically associated with the prefrontal motor cortex (purple circle)–lateral striatum–thalamus CSTC loop, as shown in Fig. 1.4.C. Gross motor hyperactivity is often more pronounced in children, and inefficient modulation within this loop would theoretically cause a child to fidget, leave his/her seat, run/climb, constantly be on the go, and have trouble playing alone. In adults, motor hyperactivity can be seen as internal restlessness and trouble sitting through meetings (more details on the difference in ADHD symptoms between children and adults can be found in Table 2.1).

Cognitive Dysfunction in ADHD Linked to Deficient Arousal

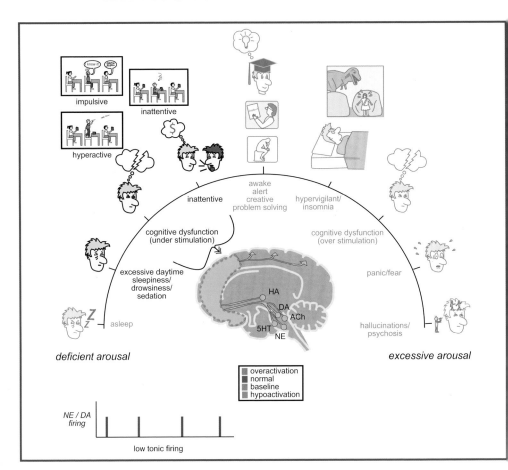

FIGURE 1.11. The underlying neurobiology of ADHD is also linked to the arousal pathways of the brain. Some patients with ADHD may have hypothetically deficient arousal networks which can lead to inefficient information processing via defective inhibitory pathways. Hypoactivity in the frontal part of the brain is associated with low tonic firing of both norepinephrine (NE) and dopamine (DA) neurons. This is the underlying hypothesis why stimulants, by bringing the activity of neurotransmitters in those circuits back to normal, can be beneficial in the treatment of ADHD.

Cognitive Dysfunction in ADHD Linked to Excessive Arousal, Stress and Comorbidity

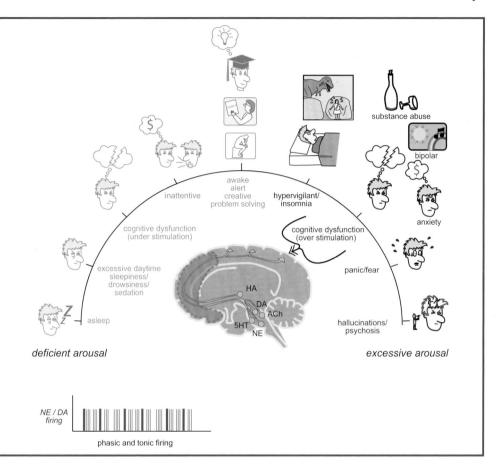

FIGURE 1.12. Excessive arousal mechanisms are theoretically as disruptive as deficient ones, since they will also lead to deteriorating signal-to-noise ratios. Hyperarousal can often be associated with chronic stress and comorbidities such as anxiety, and is characterized by increased tonic and phasic firing of prefrontal NE and DA neurons. In general, it is safe to say that in the arousal spectrum, the prefrontal cortex is "out of tune" and needs to be set back to normal. As will be shown in Chapter 4, this can be accomplished by agents other than stimulants.

ADHD: Weak NE and DA
Signals in Prefrontal Cortex

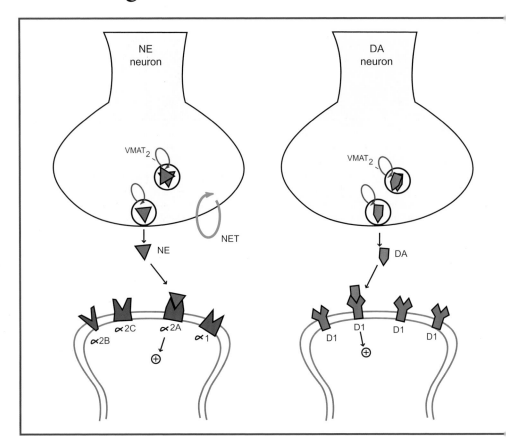

FIGURE 1.13. As has been mentioned in the previous pages, deficient signaling in DA and NE pathways is hypothesized to underlie symptoms of ADHD in some patients. Besides being a key player in the arousal pathways, the prefrontal cortex is also the main brain area where imbalances in these two neurotransmitter systems hypothetically occur in ADHD. Agents that can increase release of these two neurotransmitters, or that can lead to increased tonic firing of these neurons, will be hypothetically beneficial in patients with ADHD by increasing prefrontal activity to an optimal level.

Similar Symptoms in Different Disorders: Does It Matter?

Symptom \ Disorder	ADHD	MDD/ GAD	Narcolepsy	OSA	SW	Sleep deprivation
Inattention/ problems concentrating	+++	++	++	++	++	+++
Mood/anxiety	-	+++	-	+	-	+/-
Sleepiness	+	+	+++	+++	+++	+++
Fatigue	+	++	++	++	++	+++

ADHD: attention deficit hyperactivity disorder; GAD: generalized anxiety disorder; MDD: major depressive disorder; OSA: obstructive sleep apnea; SW: shift work

TABLE 1.1. Is inattention in ADHD any different from inattention in any other psychiatric disorder, and should it then be treated any differently? This is the question one can ask when examining the overlap of different symptoms in ADHD versus other disorders. The same brain circuits that mediate inattention in one disorder theoretically mediate inattention in other disorders (see first row in table above). Thus, treatments for inattention in one disorder may also be effective for treating inattention in another.

Impact of Genetics in ADHD

GENE	FUNCTION
DAT (dopamine transporter)	DAT clears DA from the synapse, transporting it back into the neuron
DRD 4 (D_4 receptor)	Member of the D2-like family of DA receptors; linked to G protein $G\alpha i$
DRD 5 (D_5 receptor)	Member of the D1-like family of DA receptors; linked to G protein $G\alpha s$
DBH (dopamine beta hydroxylase)	This enzyme converts DA to NE
ADRA 2A (alpha 2A receptor)	Linked to G protein G_i, thus inactivating adenylyl cyclase
SNAP 25 (synaptic protein)	Synaptosome-associated protein of 25-kDa, inhibits presynaptic P/Q- and L-type voltage-gated calcium channels
5HTTLPR (long) (5HT transporter)	Serotonin-transporter-linked polymorphic region in this gene codes for different forms of the serotonin transporter
HTR 1B (serotonin 1B receptor)	Induces presynaptic inhibition in the CNS, and has vascular effects
FADS 2 (fatty acid desaturase 2)	Desaturase enzymes regulate unsaturation of fatty acids by adding double bonds between specific carbons of the fatty acyl chain

TABLE 1.2. Genetics play an important role in the etiology of ADHD. The mean heritability of ADHD is ~75%, making this disorder as heritable, if not more, as schizophrenia. As can be seen in this table, the major genes linked to ADHD are implicated in DA neurotransmission, with additional genes relating to adrenergic and serotonergic neurotransmission as well.

Nature vs. Nurture

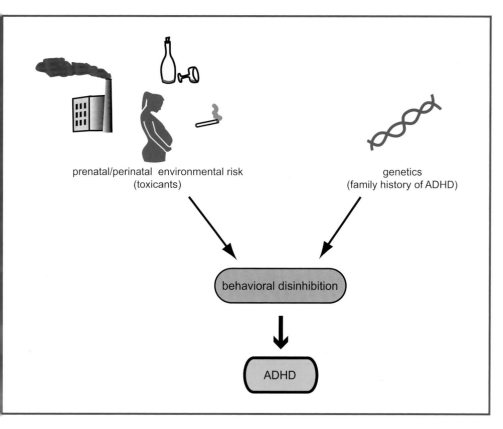

prenatal/perinatal environmental risk
(toxicants)

genetics
(family history of ADHD)

behavioral disinhibition

ADHD

FIGURE 1.14. Theoretically the modern disease model of ADHD hypothesizes that different risk factors interact to lead to behavioral disinhibition and ultimately the symptoms of ADHD. Behavioral disinhibition, which is mainly a result of genetics, has been hypothesized to be at the core of ADHD. A certain combination of external risk factors such as prenatal tobacco and alcohol exposure, hypoxia, prematurity/low birth weight, emotional status of the mother during pregnancy, duration of labor, and low-level lead exposure can also impact the genetics of ADHD. Specifically it has been shown that children with hyperactivity often had more prenatal/perinatal complications. Thus it is important to take all these factors into consideration when diagnosing and treating ADHD.

Everything You Wanted to Know About ADHD But Forgot You Wanted to Ask

Chapter 2:

ADHD Across the Ages

Objectives:

- Understand the role of synaptogenesis in the prefrontal cortex and how it relates to ADHD
- Compare and contrast the diagnosis of ADHD in children versus adolescents versus adults
- Identify the different presentations of ADHD among different age groups
- Understand the different rating scales used for diagnosing ADHD and how they apply to the various groups of patients

Synaptogenesis in Prefrontal Cortex and the Development of Executive Functions

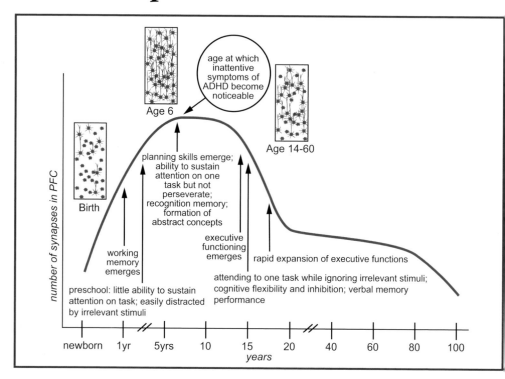

FIGURE 2.1. Synaptogenesis in the prefrontal cortex might be responsible for altered connections that could prime the brain for ADHD. Specifically, executive function develops throughout adolescence. At 1 year of age, working memory emerges. Around 3-4 years of age, children do not yet have the capability to sustain attention for long periods of time, and can be easily distracted. By age 6-7, this changes; attention can be sustained and planning can take place. This age is also characterized by "synaptic pruning," a process during which overproduced or "weak" synapses are "weeded out," thus allowing for the child's cognitive intelligence to mature. Errors in this process could hypothetically affect the further development of executive function and be one of the causes of ADHD. This timeline also represents when symptoms of ADHD often become noticeable, which is around the age of 6.

Impact of Development on ADHD

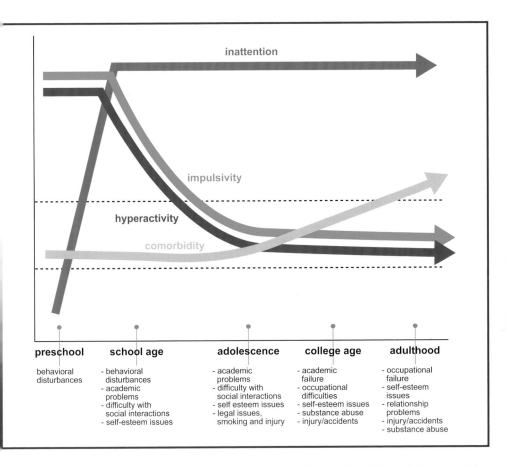

FIGURE 2.2. The evolution of symptoms across the ages shows that although hyperactivity and impulsivity are key symptoms in childhood, inattention becomes prevalent as the patient ages. Additionally, the rates of comorbidities increase over time. This could be due to the fact that the comorbidities were overlooked in children with ADHD, or because ADHD was never diagnosed in some patients presenting with anxiety or learning disabilities. One could say that "the jury is still out" on this issue.

Persistence of ADHD into Adulthood

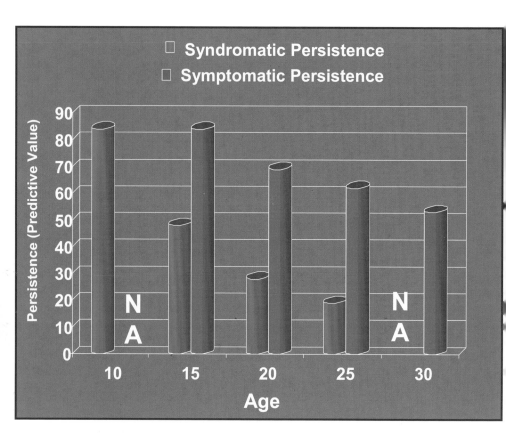

FIGURE 2.3. Although some have argued that the occurrence of ADHD diminishes with age, others would prefer to say that the symptoms of ADHD simply change over time. Specifically, symptoms such as hyperactivity are thought to diminish from childhood to adolescence to adulthood, whereas symptoms of inattention persist or even worsen. Thus, as a patient ages, s/he may no longer meet syndromatic criteria (green bars), depending on which diagnostic criteria and/or scales are used to assess the patient. However, subsyndromal symptoms may still persist and require treatment and/or monitoring (red bars). In this case symptomatic persistence is defined as loss of partial diagnostic status but without functional recovery.

Evolution of ADHD Symptoms With Age

	Childhood	Adulthood
Inattention	Difficulty sustaining attention	Difficulty sustaining attention
	Fails to pay attention to details	Makes careless errors
	Appears not to listen	Easily distracted/forgetful
	Lacks follow-through	Poor concentration
	Cannot organize	Hard to finish tasks
	Loses important items	Disorganized/misplaces items
Hyperactivity	Squirming, fidgeting	Inefficient at work
	Cannot stay seated	Internal restlessness
	Cannot wait turn	Difficulty sitting through meetings
	Runs/climbs excessively	Works more than one job
	"on the go"/driven by motor	Self-selects very active job
	Talks excessively	Overwhelmed/talks excessively
Impulsivity	Blurts out answers	Impulsive job changes
	Cannot wait in line	Drives too fast
	Intrudes/interrupts others	Interrupts others/easily frustrated

TABLE 2.1. The symptoms of inattention, hyperactivity, and impulsivity will have different faces in children vs. adults. This table aims to show the parallels between the symptoms of ADHD in children and adults and give equivalents for each behavior. To make a proper diagnosis of ADHD in these different age groups, it is important for physicians to keep this in mind as they interview their patients.

Screening and Rating Scales: Children

SCALE	NOTES
Attention Deficit Disorders Evaluation Scale (ADDES-3)	Ages 4-18
Brown Attention-Deficit Disorder Scales for Children	Ages 12-18
Conner's Parent Rating Scale (CPRS)	Scale is factor-structured, reliable and has criterion validity
ADHD Rating Scale *	Ages 6-12
Vanderbilt ADHD Diagnostic Rating Scales	Ages 6-12; includes a parent and teacher form
SNAP-IV Rating Scale - Revised (SNAP-IV-R) *	Ages 6-18; includes parent and teacher rating scale
ADD-H: Comprehensive Teacher's Rating Scale (ACTeRs)	Ages 6-14; includes a parent form
Attention Deficit/Hyperactivity Disorder Test (ADHDT)	Ages 3-23
ADHD Symptom Checklist-4 (ADHD-SC4)	Ages 3-18
Copeland Symptom Checklist for Attention Deficit Disorder	Children, adolescents
Werry-Weiss-Peters Activity Rating Scale	Children and adolescents; four parent forms and four school forms
SWAN Rating Scale *	Children and adolescents; results can differentiate between ADHD type
Test of Everyday Attention for Children (TEA-Ch)	Ages 6-16; assesses different attentional capacities

TABLE 2.2. There are many rating scales to choose from when interviewing children and adolescents with psychiatric disorders such as ADHD. This table gives an overview of these scales in terms of what ages they are appropriate for and what is specific about them. The * designates the rating scales that can be found in the Appendix.

Screening and Rating Scales: Adults

SCALE	NOTES
Conners Adult Attention Deficit/Hyperactivity Disorder Rating Scale (CAARS)	Three versions: investigator-rated, observer-rated, and self-rated
Brown Attention Deficit Disorder Scale for Adults (BADDS)	Emphasis on inattention rather than hyperactivity/impulsivity; developed before DSM-IV ADHD criteria
Wender Utah Rating Scale (WURS) *	Tool used to assess ADHD retrospectively
Childhood/current ADHD Symptom Scale	Childhood scale: 18 items relating to adult patient when s/he was a child Current scale: 18 items relating to current adult situation
Adult Rating Scale	Checklist assessing ADHD symptoms according to DSM-IV
Adult ADHD Self-Report Scale (ASRS-v1.1) *	Has two parts; first part is a screening test; second part more in-depth questions
Copeland Symptom Checklist for Attention Deficit Disorder	Adult version
College ADHD Response Evaluation (CARE)	Ages 17-23
Attention-Deficit Scales for Adults (ADSA)	54 items
	Ages 4-80+

TABLE 2.3. There are also many rating scales to choose from when interviewing adults with probable ADHD. This table gives an overview of the screening and rating scales available to physicians and patients. Some of the scales rate current symptoms and childhood symptoms to determine whether the disorder had been there in childhood or whether the person might have been able to compensate for it. The * designates the rating scales that can be found in the Appendix.

Everything You Wanted to Know About ADHD But Forgot You Wanted to Ask

Chapter 3:

Comorbidities of ADHD

Objectives:

- Understand the prevalence of comorbidities in children and adolescents with ADHD
- Understand the prevalence of comorbidities in adults with ADHD
- Recognize the importance of treating all disorders

Comorbidities in Children

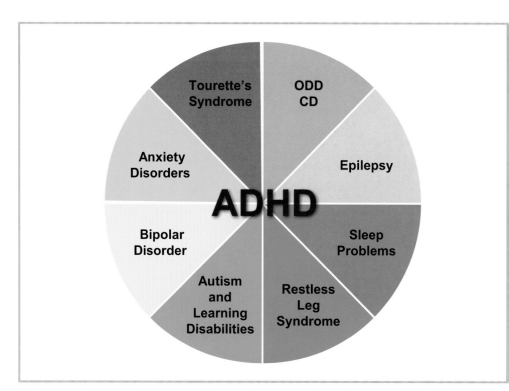

FIGURE 3.1. It has been suggested that ADHD, Tourette's syndrome, and restless leg syndrome may be comorbid in children and that iron deficiency could be one of the underlying causes. Additionally, 50% of school-aged children with ADHD also meet the DSM-IV criteria for oppositional defiant disorder (ODD) or conduct disorder (CD). It becomes clear that no matter what the comorbidity is, children with ADHD can be further burdened. It is therefore imperative to properly diagnose them and treat them appropriately.

The Connection Between Sleep Problems and ADHD

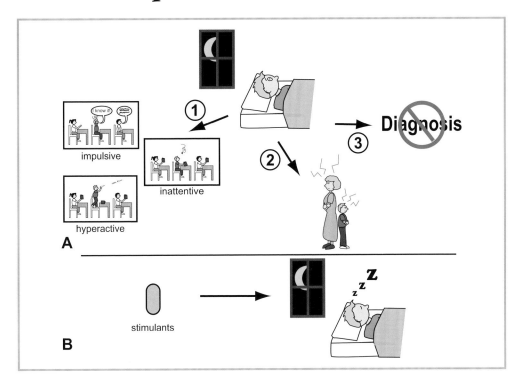

FIGURE 3.2. (A) Twenty-five percent to 55% of parents complain of sleep problems in their children with ADHD. These range from difficulty falling asleep, resistance to bedtime, nighttime awakenings, to difficulty waking up. Adults with ADHD are not immune to sleep problems and exhibit similar symptoms as children. Improving sleep problems can have multiple benefits, because (1) sleep problems can worsen the symptoms of ADHD and other related mood disorders, and (2) sleep problems can be especially distressing to the child/adult and the family, and therefore improving them can increase the quality-of-life for everyone involved. (3) Sleep disorders that result in lack of sleep, daytime sleepiness and fragmented sleep can lead to mood alterations and issues with attention and behavior. These sleep disturbances can look like ADHD, and lead to the misdiagnosis of ADHD in children/adults that exhibit behavioral disturbances resulting from sleep issues. (B) The treatment of ADHD with stimulants has actually been shown to increase sleep efficiency and the subjective feeling of restorative value of sleep in adults. Thus if stimulants are taken properly, they will improve sleep, further emphasizing the connection between sleep and ADHD.

Comorbidities in Adults

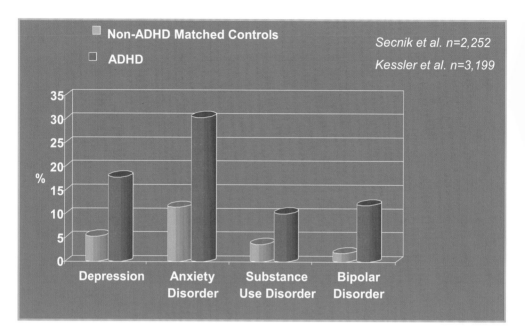

FIGURE 3.3. Comorbidities in adults take on a different face than in children, but can have the same devastating effects, both for the patients and for society as a whole. Patients with ADHD might need more time to finish their projects than their non-ADHD counterparts. If they are further impaired by anxiety disorders or substance use, their productivity can be further decreased. Additionally, as adults with ADHD have a higher number of traffic citations and accidents with bodily injury, this can be devastating if they are also suffering from substance use disorder (SUD). Any comorbidity will need to be treated in conjunction with ADHD, if "full remission" in both disorders is expected.

Bi-Directional Overlap Between ADHD and Substance Use Disorders

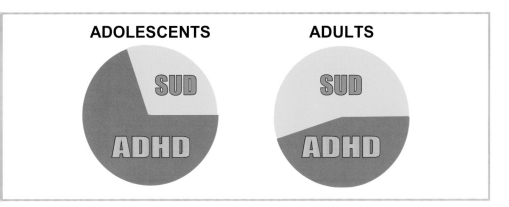

FIGURE 3.4. Patients with ADHD can have many comorbidities, and in adults substance use disorder (SUD) is one of the most important ones (see Fig. 3.3). In a patient population with ADHD as the primary disorder, 15%-30% of adolescents have been shown to have SUD, whereas 35%-55% of adults have SUD.

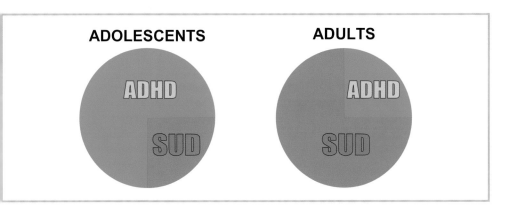

FIGURE 3.5. Conversely, in a patient population with SUD as the primary disorder, 40%-75% of adolescents also have ADHD, whereas 15%-25% of adults also exhibit ADHD symptoms. This also emphasizes that some symptoms such as impulsivity and risk taking are underlying both disorders. When comorbid, these two disorders can have a huge impact on the treatment of each other, and therefore both need to be addressed simultaneously.

What Should Be Treated First?

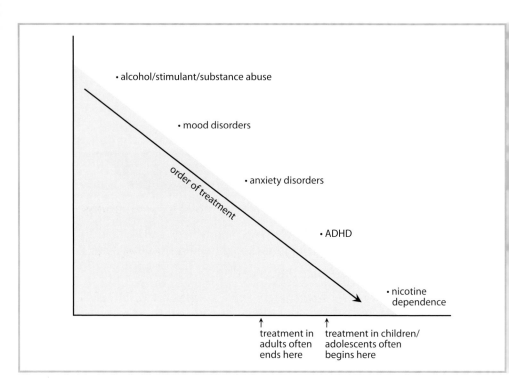

FIGURE 3.6. So what should a psychopharmacologist do with a patient with ADHD and comorbid disorders? Once the proper diagnosis has been reached, it is imperative to treat all disorders appropriately, and in terms of highest degree of impairment. This might mean that in one patient it is necessary to first stabilize the alcohol abuse, while in another patient the symptoms of ADHD might be more impairing than the underlying anxiety disorder. Additionally, some medications used to treat these disorders could exacerbate the comorbid ailment. Thus, care needs to be taken when choosing the appropriate treatment. An individualized treatment plan should therefore be established for each patient, depending on his/her symptomatic portfolio.

Chapter 4

The Treatment of ADHD

Objectives:

- Identify the different agents, and their formulations, used to treat ADHD
- Understand the mechanism of action of stimulant and non-stimulant medications
- Identify the best treatment strategies for ADHD in children versus adolescents versus adults
- Ascertain the best treatment approaches and outcome for each patient

ADHD in Children and Adolescents vs. Adults

Children 6-12 Adolescents 13-17	Adults > 18
7%-8% prevalence	4%-5% prevalence
easy to diagnose	hard to diagnose • inaccurate retrospective recall of onset • onset by age 7 too stringent • late-onset same genetics, comorbidity and impairment
diagnosed by pediatricians, child pyschiatrists, child psychologists	diagnosed by adult psychiatrists, adult mental and medical health professionals
high levels of identification and treatment >50% treated	low levels of identification and treatment < 20% treated
stimulants prescribed first-, second-line	Non-stimulants often prescribed first-line
2/3 of stimulant use is under age 18; most of this under age 13	1/3 of stimulant use is age 18 or over
1/3 of atomoxetine use is under age 18; most of this over the age of 12	2/3 of atomoxetine use is age 18 or over

TABLE 4.1. This table recaps the main differences between the symptoms, diagnosis, and treatment of ADHD in children/adolescents versus adults, and exemplifies the stigma of treating adults with stimulants. Even though properly dosed stimulants can be as efficacious in adults as they are in children, many physicians prefer to refrain from prescribing stimulants in a group that could be diverting the medication. In support of this decision, there are many good non-stimulant medications that have proven beneficial in treating ADHD in adults and in children. This chapter will elaborate on all drugs available and how they hypothetically can lead to "remission."

Treatment Choices Differ
with the Age of the Patient

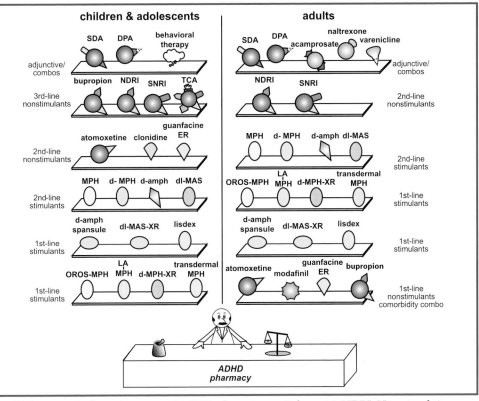

SDA: serotonin dopamine antagonist; DPA: dopamine partial agonist; NDRI: Norepinephrine dopamine reuptake inhibitor; SNRI: serotonin norepinephrine reuptake inhibitor; TCA: tricyclic antidepressant; MPH: methylphenidate

FIGURE 4.1. For children with ADHD the most common treatments include "slow-dose" extended-release stimulants, while immediate-release stimulants, atomoxetine, and alpha 2A agonists are used if this first treatment proves ineffective. Antidepressants with noradrenergic properties represent the next step in case symptoms persist, and adjunctive options can include atypical antipsychotics or behavioral therapy. For adults with ADHD, the non-stimulants such as atomoxetine, guanfacine ER, bupropion, or perhaps modafinil are a preferred first choice of treatment, followed by slow-dose, extended-release stimulants or prodrugs. Immediate-release stimulants and noradrenergic antidepressants are second-line options, whereas atypical antipsychotics are adjunctive options, as well as drug abuse treatments for patients with addiction/dependence. The following pages will describe the mechanisms of action of the main drugs used in ADHD.

Use of ADHD Medication by Agent and Formulation

Medication type	Pediatric (Age 0 to 19)		Adult (Age 20 and up)	
	2000	2005	2000	2005
Agent (immediate-release)				
Amphetamine mix	34.1	32.4	24.5	43.4
Dextroamphetamine	9.2	1.4	14.5	6.3
Methamphetamine	0	0	0.4	0.2
Methylphenidate	55.8	46.9	54.9	34.5
Dexmethylphenidate	--	2.5	--	0.9
Atomoxetine	--	16.7	--	13.7
Formulation				
Extended-release	8.9	68.3	6.1	43.7
Immediate-release	91.1	31.7	93.9	56.3

TABLE 4.2. This table reports the use of the different ADHD medications as a percentage of the total days' supply of dispensed medications for the pediatric age group (ages 0 to 19) and the adult age group (age 20 and up). The use of extended-release medications has seen a surge between 2000 and 2005, and at the same time the use of immediate-release compounds, in both the pediatric and adult groups, has declined significantly. Dexmethylphenidate and atomoxetine were first approved by the FDA in late 2001 and late 2002, respectively. Note: The numbers may not add up because of rounding.

Medications Used in ADHD

Brand Name	Generic Name
Amphetamine	
Adderall	Immediate-release d, l-amphetamine
Adderall XR	Extended-release d, l-amphetamine
Dexedrine	Immediate-release d-amphetamine
Dexedrine Spansules	Sustained-release d-amphetamine
Vyvanse	Lisdexamfetamine dimesylate
Methylphenidate	
Ritalin, Methylin	Immediate-release racemic methylphenidate
Focalin	Immediate-release d-methylphenidate
Ritalin SR, Methylin SR	Sustained-release racemic methylphenidate
Concerta	OROS technology racemic methylphenidate
Focalin XR	SODAS microbeads d-methylphenidate
Daytrana	Methylphenidate transdermal multipolymeric patch
Ritalin LA	SODAS microbeads racemic methylphenidate
Metadate-CD	Time-release beads racemic methylphenidate
Non-stimulant drugs	
Strattera, Attentin	Atomoxetine
Tenex	Guanfacine immediate-release
Intuniv*	Guanfacine extended-release
Wellbutrin, Zyban	Bupropion
Provigil	Modafinil

TABLE 4.3. The stimulant medications used for the treatment of ADHD come in two flavors: amphetamine and methylphenidate. They are sold under many different brand names, each of which have a slightly different formulation. This table will hopefully help clinicians match the brand name to the generic name of the stimulant medication currently on the market. The non-stimulant medications, on the other hand, are to date easier to differentiate. *not yet approved for ADHD, but in late stages of clinical development in U.S.

Specifics of ADHD Medications

Drug	Peak (hours)	Duration (hours)	FDA-Approved
Amphetamine			
Adderall	3	6-9	3-12
Adderall XR	7	6-10	6-17, adults
Dexedrine	3	4-6	3-16
Dexedrine Spansules	4	6-10	3-16
Vyvanse	3.5	10-12	6-12, adults
Methylphenidate			
Ritalin, Methylin	1-2	4-5	6-12
Focalin	1-2	4-5	6-17
Ritalin SR, Methylin SR	5	8	6-15
Concerta	6-8	12	6-17
Focalin XR	Biphasic: 1-2 and 6-7	12-16	6-17, adults
Daytrana	7-10	12	6-12
Ritalin LA		>5	6-12
Metadate-CD	Biphasic: 1-2 and 4-5	6-8	6-15
Non-stimulants			
Strattera, Attentin	1-2	20	6-18, adults
Tenex	1-4	24	Children and adults
Intuniv*	~ 12	>24	Children and adults
Wellbutrin, Zyban	10-17	14-24	18-83
Provigil	2-4	15-30	adults

TABLE 4.4. An overview of the characteristics of the different formulations presented in Table 4.3, the time at which they peak, and their duration of action. The FDA-approved ages are also listed; even though some of these drugs are not approved for all age groups, many clinical studies have shown them to be efficacious for different ages as well. *not yet approved for ADHD, but in late stages of clinical development in U.S.

Slow-Dose Stimulants Amplify Tonic NE and DA Signals

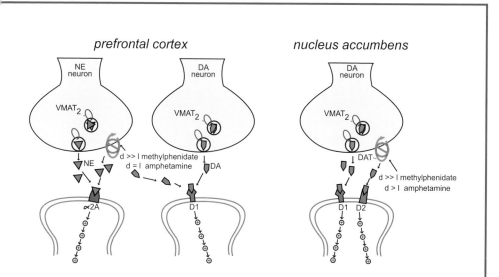

slow-dose stimulants

OROS - methylphenidate; LA - methylphenidate; XR - d-methylphenidate; transdermal methylphenidate; d-amphetamine spansules; XR - d,l mixed amphetamine salts; XXR - d,l mixed amphetamine salts; prodrug d-amphetamine (lisdexamfetamine)

FIGURE 4.2. Hypothetically, whether a drug has abuse potential depends on how it affects the DA pathway. In other words, the pharmacodynamic and pharmacokinetic properties of stimulants affect their therapeutic as well as their potential abuse profiles. Extended-release formulations of oral stimulants, the transdermal methylphenidate patch and the new prodrug lisdexamfetamine are all considered "slow-dose" stimulants and may amplify tonic NE and DA signals, presumed to be low in some patients with ADHD. These agents block the norepinephrine transporter (NET) in the prefrontal cortex and the DA transporter (DAT) in the nucleus accumbens. Hypothetically, the "slow-dose" stimulants occupy NET in the prefrontal cortex with slow enough onset and for long enough duration that they enhance tonic NE and DA signaling via alpha 2A and D1 postsynaptic receptors, respectively, but they do not occupy DAT quickly or extensively enough in the nucleus accumbens to increase phasic signaling via D2 receptors. This hypothetically suggests reduced abuse potential.

Pulsatile Stimulants Amplify Tonic and Phasic NE and DA Signals

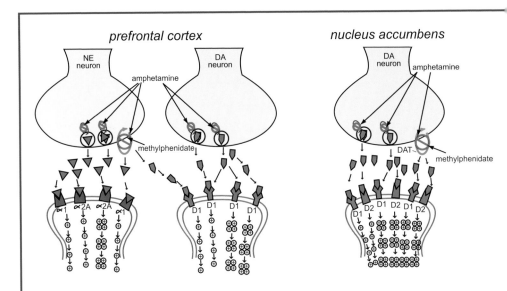

pulsatile stimulants
oral immediate release; intravenous; intranasal; smoked; d-amphetamine; d,l amphetamine salts; methylphenidate; d-methylphenidate; cocaine; methamphetamine

FIGURE 4.3. Immediate-release oral stimulants — similarly to intravenous, smoked or snorted stimulants (which are considered pulsatile stimulants) — lead to a rapid increase in NE and DA levels. Rapidly increasing the phasic neuronal firing of DA and NE is associated with euphoria and abuse. This figure shows that both the pharmacodynamic and pharmacokinetic properties of stimulants can affect both their therapeutic and abuse profiles. In contrast to methylphenidate, high doses of amphetamine lead to blockade of both DAT and the vesicular monoamine transporter (VMAT), thus leading to displacement and massive release of DA. This increased release of DA may also contribute to the abuse potential of immediate-release formulations of stimulants, suggesting phasic as well as tonic DA signals.

Atomoxetine in ADHD with Weak Prefrontal NE and DA Signals

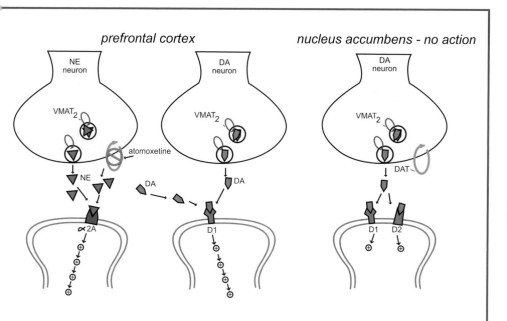

FIGURE 4.4. The non-stimulant atomoxetine can have therapeutic effects in ADHD without abuse potential. This norepinephrine reuptake blocker causes NE and DA levels to increase n the prefrontal cortex, where inactivation of both of these neurotransmitters is largely due to NET (on the left). At the same time the lack of norepinephrine transporters in the nucleus accumbens prevents atomoxetine from increasing NE or DA levels in that brain rea, thus reducing the risk of abuse (on the right).

ADHD, Stress and Comorbidities

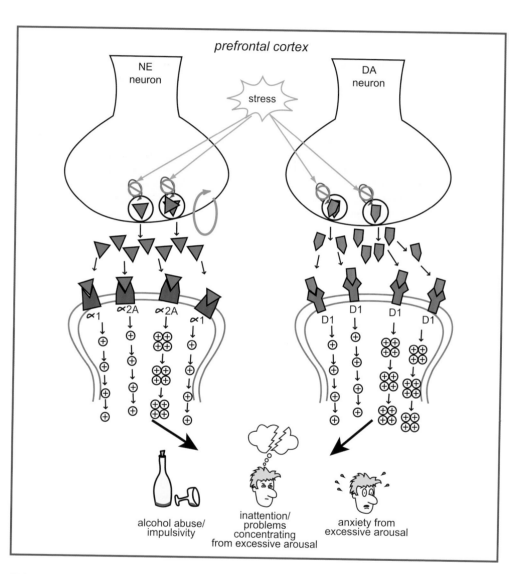

FIGURE 4.5. Non-treated adults with ADHD can often be stressed as they are trying to deal with their disorder while at the same time trying to accomplish as much as their peers. Unfortunately, stress can activate NE and DA circuits in the prefrontal cortex and thus cause an excess of phasic NE and DA firing. This excessive NE and DA neurotransmission may be the underpinnings of the development of drug and alcohol abuse, impulsivity, inattention, and anxiety, all comorbid with ADHD. This again emphasizes the notion that treatment of all disorders is necessary to ascertain good patient outcome.

Chronic Treatment with Atomoxetine in ADHD with Excessive Prefrontal NE and DA Signals

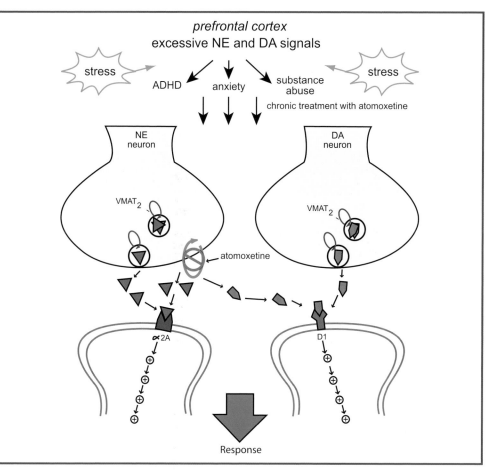

FIGURE 4.6. Stress combined with excessive NE and DA signaling can lead to ADHD, anxiety, or substance abuse. One way to reduce excessive stimulation could be to desensitize postsynaptic DA and NE receptors, and thus allow the neurons to return to normal tonic firing over time. By continuously blocking the NE transporter, atomoxetine has the capability to do this. The "big picture" ramification of such a treatment could be the reduction of the overactivity of the HPA axis, and possibly the reversal of stress-related brain atrophy or the induction of neurogenesis. All of these might then lead to a decrease in anxiety, a decrease in heavy drinking, and a reduction in relapses.

Regulation of NE Pathways by Alpha 2A Agonist: Guanfacine ER and Clonidine

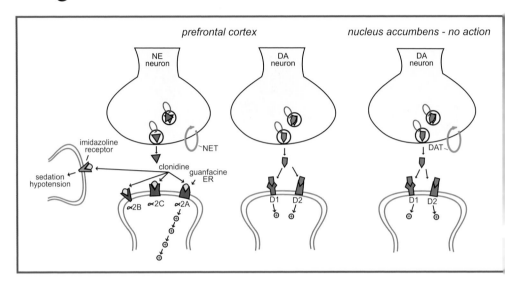

FIGURE 4.7. Alpha 2 adrenergic receptors are present in high concentrations in the prefrontal cortex, but only in low concentrations in the nucleus accumbens. It has been suggested that alpha 2A adrenergic receptors mediate the inattentive, hyperactive, and impulsive symptoms of ADHD, and that other alpha 2 adrenergic receptors may have different functions. In ADHD, alpha 2 adrenergic agonists such as clonodine, guanfacine, and guanfacine ER — by stimulating postsynaptic receptors — can increase NE signaling to normal levels (Fig. 4.8). The lack of action at postsynaptic DA receptors parallels their lack of abuse potential.

The nonselective alpha 2 adrenergic agonist, clonidine, binds to 2A, 2B, and 2C receptors. However, it also binds to imidazoline receptors, which contribute to its sedating and hypotensive effects. Although the actions of clonidine at alpha 2A receptors exhibit therapeutic potential for ADHD, its actions at other receptors may increase side effects.

The selective alpha 2A receptor agonist guanfacine, on the other hand, exhibits therapeutic efficacy with a reduced side effect profile compared to clonidine. A controlled-release formulation of guanfacine (guanfacine ER, Intuniv) is in late stage clinical development for ADHD in the U.S.

Enhancing Arousal in the Prefrontal Cortex: How It Treats ADHD

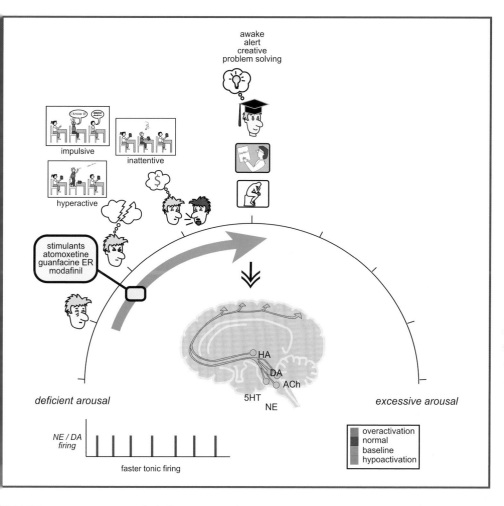

FIGURE 4.8. In patients with deficient arousal (Fig. 1.11), agents such as stimulants, atomoxetine, guanfacine ER, and modafinil can increase the drive of the arousal network by increasing the levels of DA and NE (two arousal neurotransmitters). This will hypothetically lead to an amplification of their tonic firing rate, which in turn will increase the efficiency of information processing in the prefrontal cortex and thereby improve symptoms of inattention, impulsivity, and hyperactivity.

Desensitizing Arousal in the Prefrontal Cortex: How It Treats ADHD

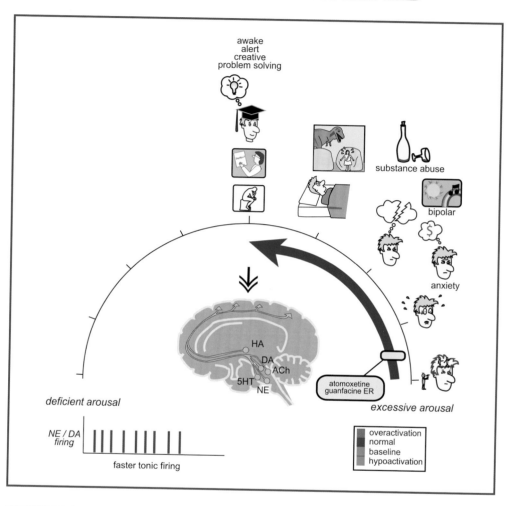

FIGURE 4.9. In patients with excessive arousal (Fig. 1.12), agents such as atomoxetine or guanfacine can lead to desensitized postsynaptic DA and NE receptors, and this may over time lead to a decrease in excessive arousal by reestablishing tonic firing in these neurons. Atomoxetine and guanfacine are two drugs that normally have tonic actions on DA and NE, and thus they may be able to reset the neurons by continuously blocking the NE transporter, or by continuously acting at alpha 2A adrenergic receptors, respectively.

Psychosocial Therapies in Adults

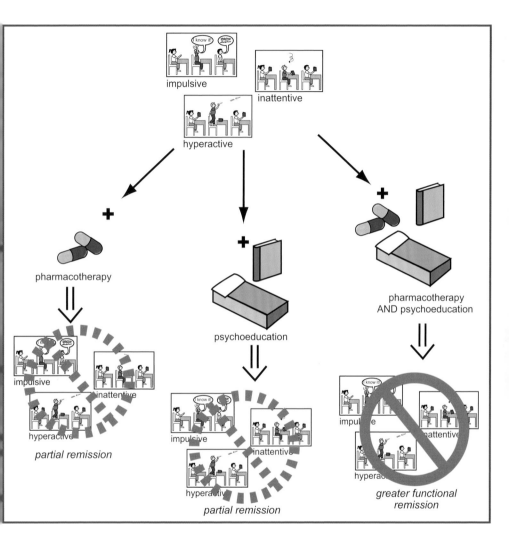

FIGURE 4.10. There is growing awareness among clinicians of the need to offer psychological treatment for ADHD patients, especially because half of adults with ADHD cannot take medications, do not respond to medications, or experience lingering side effects. The American, Canadian, and British practice guidelines all recommend that medication treatment be complemented by psychoeducation, support, and other nonpharmacological interventions.

Summary

- Patients with ADHD rarely grow out of it; they might learn how to compensate for the disorder, but under the surface the symptoms usually remain.

- ADHD has many different faces; depending on the patient's gender and age.

- Different rating scales are available for the different age groups of patients.

- ADHD is often not a stand-alone disorder; it is often comorbid with Tourette's, anxiety, substance use, or sleep disorders.

- Different stimulant and non-stimulant medications are available for the treatment of ADHD, and it is important to know how they mechanistically improve the symptoms of ADHD.

- Understanding the difference between stimulant drug formulations will be helpful to the physician to better treat their patients.

- Individualized treatment will ascertain the best possible outcome for each patient, depending on age, comorbid disorder, and side effect profile of the medication.

Abbreviations

5HTTLPR	5HT transport (long)
ACC	Anterior cingulate cortex
ADHD	Attention deficit hyperactivity disorder
ADRA 2A	Alpha 2A adrenergic receptor
CD	Conduct disorder
CSTC	Cortical-striatal-thalamic-cortical
DA	Dopamine
DAT	Dopamine transporter
DBH	Dopamine beta hydroxylase
DLPFC	Dorsolateral prefrontal cortex
DRD D4	Dopamine receptor D4
DRD D5	Dopamine receptor D5
FADS2	Fatty acid desaturase 2
GAD	Generalized anxiety disorder
HTR 1B	Serotonin 1B receptor
MDD	Major depressive disorder
NAcc	Nucleus accumbens
NDRI	Norepinephrine dopamine reuptake inhibitor
NE	Norepinephrine
NET	Norepinephrine transporter
ODD	Oppositional defiant disorder
OFC	Orbital frontal cortex
OSA	Obstructive sleep apnea
SNAP 25	Synaptosome-associated protein of 25kD
SNRI	Serotonin norepinephrine reuptake inhibitor
SUD	Substance use disorder
SW	Shift work
TCA	Tricyclic antidepressant

Suggested Readings

Allen AJ, Kurlan RM, Gilbert DL et al. Atomoxetine treatment in children and adolescents with ADHD and comorbid tic disorders. Neurology 2005;65:1941–9.

Arnsten AFT. Fundamentals of attention deficit/hyperactivity disorder: circuits and pathways. J Clin Psychiatry 2006;67:Suppl 8, 7–12.

Arnsten AFT. Stimulants: therapeutic actions in ADHD. Neuropsychopharmacology 2006;31:2376–83.

Arnsten AFT and Li BM. Neurobiology of executive functions: catecholamine influences on prefrontal cortical functions. Biol Psychiatry 2005;57:1377–84.

Avery RA, Franowicz JS, Phil M et al. The alpha 2A adrenoceptor agonist, guanfacine, increases regional cerebral blood flow in dorsolateral prefrontal cortex of monkeys performing a spatial working memory task. Neuropsychopharmacology 2000;23:240–9.

Bellgrove MA, Hawi Z, Kirley A et al. Association between dopamine transporter (DAT1) genotype, left-side inattention, and an enhanced response to methylphenidate in attention deficit hyperactivity disorder. Neuropsychopharmacology 2005;30:2290–7.

Berridge CW, Devilbiss DM and Rzejewski ME et al. Methylphenidate preferentially increases catecholamine neurotransmission within the prefrontal cortex at low doses that enhance cognitive function. Biol Psychiatry 2006;60:1111–20.

Biederman J. Impact of comorbidity in adults with attention deficit/hyperactivity disorder. J Clin Psychiatry 2004;65:Suppl 3, 3–7.

Biederman J, Mick E, Surman C et al. A randomized, placebo-controlled trial of OROS methylphenidate in adults with attention deficit/hyperactivity disorder. Biol Psychiatry 2006;59:829–35.

Biederman J, Monuteaux MC, Mick E et al. Psychopathology in females with attention deficit/hyperactivity disorder: a controlled, five year prospective study. Biol Psychiatry 2006;60:1098–105.

Biederman J, Monuteaux MC, Mick E et al. Is cigarette smoking a gateway to alcohol and illicit drug use disorders? A study of youths with and without attention deficit hyperactivity disorder. Biol Psychiatry 2006;59:258–64.

Biederman J, Petty CR, Fried R et al. Stability of executive function deficits into young adult years: a prospective longitudinal follow-up study of grown up males with ADHD. Acta Psychiatr Scand 2007;116:129–36.

Biederman J, Swanson JM, Wigal SB et al. A comparison of once daily and divided doses of modafinil in children with attention deficit/hyperactivity disorder: a randomized, double blind and placebo controlled study. J Clin Psychiatry 2006;67:727–35.

Bush G, Valera EM and Seidman LJ. Functional neuroimaging of attention deficit/ hyperactivity disorder: a review and suggested future directions. Biol Psychiatry 2005;57:1273–84.

Castle L, Aubert RE, Verbrugge RR et al. Trends in medication treatment for ADHD. J Atten Disord 2007;10:335-42.

Carpenter LL, Milosavljevic N, Schecter JM et al. Augmentation with open label atomoxetine for partial or nonresponse to antidepressants. J Clin Psychiatry 2005;66(10):1234–8.

Cortese S, Konofal E, Yateman N et al. Sleep and alertness in children with attention deficit/hyperactivity disorder: a systematic review of the literature. Sleep 2006;29(4):504–11.

Cortese S, Lecendreux M, Bernardina BD et al. Attention-deficit/hyperactivity disorder, Tourette's syndrome, and restless legs syndrome: The iron hypothesis. Medical Hypotheses 2008;70(6):1128-32.

Coull JT, Nobre AC and Frith CD. The noradrenergic alpha 2 agonist clonidine modulates behavioural and neuroanatomical correlates of human attentional orienting and alerting. Cereb Cortex 2001;11:73–84.

Faraone SV. Advances in the genetics and neurobiology of attention deficit hyperactivity disorder. Biol Psychiatry 2006;60:1025–7.

Faraone SV, Biederman J, Doyle A et al. Neuropsychological studies of late onset and subthreshold diagnoses of adult attention deficit/hyperactivity disorder. Biol Psychiatry 2006;60:1081–7.

Faraone SV, Biederman J, Spencer T et al. Diagnosing adult attention deficit hyperactivity disorder: are late onset and subthreshold diagnoses valid? Am J Psychiatry 2006;163(10):1720–9.

Fischman AJ and Madras BK. The neurobiology of attention-deficit/hyperactivity disorder. Biol Psychiatry 2005;57:1374–6.

Franowicz JS and Arnsten AFT. Actions of alpha 2 noradrenergic agonists on spatial working memory and blood pressure in rhesus monkeys appear to be mediated by the same receptor subtype. Psychopharmacology 2002;162:304–12.

Franowicz JS, Phil M and Arnsten AFT. Treatment with the noradrenergic alpha-2 agonist conidine, but not diazepam, improves spatial working memory in normal young rhesus monkeys. Neuropsychopharmacology 1999;21:611–21.

Gibbs SE and Depositor M. Individual capacity differences predict working memory performance and prefrontal activity following dopamine receptor stimulation. Cogn Affective Behav Neurosci 2005;5(2):212–21.

Harvey EA, Friedman-Weieneth JL, Goldstein LH et al. Examining subtypes of behavior problems among 3-year-old children, Part I: Investigating validity of subtypes and biological risk factors. J Abnorm Child Psychol 2007;35:97-110.

Hazell P. Do adrenergically active drugs have a role in the first-line treatment of attention-deficit/hyperactivity disorder? Expert Opin Pharmacother 2005;12:1989–98.

Jakala P, Riekkinen M, Sirvio J et al. Guanfacine, but not clonidine, improves planning and working memory performance in humans. Neuropsychopharmacology 1999;20:460–70.

Jakala P, Riekkinen M, Sirvio J et al. Clonidine, but not guanfacine, impairs choice reaction time performance in young healthy volunteers. Neuropsychopharmacology 1999;21:495–502.

Jakala P, Sirvio J, Riekkinen M et al. Guanfacine and clonidine, alpha 2 agonists, improve paired associates learning, but not delayed matching to sample, in humans. Neuropsychopharmacology 1999;20:119–30.

essler RC, Adler L, Barkley R et al. The prevalence and correlates of adult ADHD in the United States: results from the National Comorbidity Survey replication. Am J Psychiatry 2006;163:716–23.

ollins SH, McClernon J and Fuemmeler BF. Association between smoking and attention deficit/hyperactivity disorder symptoms in a population-based sample of young adults. Arch Gen Psychiatry 2005;62:1142–7.

ahey BB, Pelham WE, Loney J et al. Instability of the DSMIV subtypes of ADHD from preschool through elementary school. Arch Gen Psychiatry 2005;62:896–902.

evy R and Goldman-Rakic PS. Association of storage and processing functions in the dorsolateral prefrontal cortex of the nonhuman primate. J Neurosci 1999;19(12):5149–58.

u J, Jhou T and Saper CB. Identification of wake active dopaminergic neurons in the ventral periaqueductal gray matter. J Neurosci 2006;26(1):193–202.

Ma CL, Arnsten AFT and Li BM. Locomotor hyperactivity induced by blockade of prefrontal cortical alpha 2 adrenoceptors in monkeys. Biol Psychiatry 2005;57:192–5.

Madras BK, MillerGM and Fischman AJ. The dopamine transporter and attention deficit/hyperactivity disorder. Biol Psychiatry 2005;57:1397–409.

Mattay VS, Callicott JH, Bertolino A et al. Effects of dextroamphetamine on cognitive performance and cortical activation. NeuroImage 2000;12:268–75.

McGough JJ, Wigal SB, Abikoff H et al. A randomized, double-blind, placebo-controlled, laboratory classroom assessment of methylphenidate transdermal system in children with ADHD. J Atten Disord 2006;9(3):476–85.

Mick E, Faraone SV and Biederman J. Age-dependent expression of attention-deficit/hyperactivity disorder symptoms. Psychiatric Clinics of North America 2004;27(2):215-24.

Nigg JT. ADHD, lead exposure and prevention: how much lead or how much evidence is needed? Expert Rev Neurotherapeutics 2008;8(4):519-21.

Nutt DJ, Fone K, Asherson P et al. Evidence-based guidelines for management of attention-deficit/hyperactivity disorder in adolescents in transition to adult services and in adults: recommendations from the British Association for Psychopharmacology. J Psychopharm 2007;21(1):10-41.

Pliszka SR. The neuropsychopharmacology of attention deficit/hyperactivity disorder. Biol Psychiatry 2005;57:1385–90.

Randall DC, Fleck NL, Shneerson JM et al. The cognitive enhancing properties of modafinil are limited in non-sleep deprived middle-aged volunteers. Pharmacol Biochem Behav 2004;77:547–55.

Randall DC, Shneerson JM and File SE. Cognitive effects of modafinil in student volunteers may depend on IQ. Pharmacol Biochem Behav 2005;82:133–9.

Randall DC, Shneerson JM, Plaha KK et al. Modafinil affects mood, but not cognitive function, in healthy young volunteers. Hum Psychopharmacol 2003;18:163–73.

Randall DC, Viswanath A, Bharania P et al. Does modafinil enhance cognitive performance in young volunteers who are not sleep deprived? J Clin Psychopharmacol 2005;25(2):175–9.

Reimherr FW, Williams ED, Strong RE et al. A Double-blind, placebo-controlled crossover study of osmotic release oral system methylphenidate in adults with ADHD with assessment of oppositional and emotional dimensions of the disorder. J Clin Psychiatry 2007;68(1):93–101.

Research Units on Pediatric Psychopharmacology Autism Network. Randomized, controlled, crossover trial of methylphenidate in pervasive developmental disorders with hyperactivity. Arch Gen Psychiatry 2005;62:1266–74.

Schmitz M, Denardin D, Silva TL et al. Association between alpha-2a-adrenergic receptor gene and ADHD inattentive type. Biol Psychiatry 2006;60:1028–33.

Secnik K, Swensen A and Lage MJ. Comorbidities and costs of adult patients diagnosed with attention-deficit/hyperactivity disorder. Pharmacogenomics 2005;23(1):93-102.

Seidman LJ, Valera EM, Makris N et al. Dorsolateral prefrontal and anterior cingulate cortex volumetric abnormalities in adults with attention deficit/ hyperactivity disorder identified by magnetic resonance imaging. Biol Psychiatry 2006;60:1071–80.

Shafritz KM, Marchione KE, Gore JC et al. The effects of methylphenidate on neural systems of attention in attention deficit hyperactivity disorder. Am J Psychiatry 2004;161(11):1990–7.

Shaw P, Gornick M, Lerch J et al. Polymorphisms of the dopamine D4 receptor, clinical outcome, and cortical structure in attention deficit/hyperactivity disorder. Arch Gen Psychiatry 2007;64(8):921–31.

Smith AB, Taylor E, Brammer M et al. Task-specific hypoactivation in prefrontal and temporoparietal brain regions during motor inhibition and task switching in mediation naive children and adolescents with attention deficit hyperactivity disorder. Am J Psychiatry 2006;163:1044–51.

Solanta MV. Dopamine dysfunction in AD/HD: integrating clinical and basic neuroscience research. Behav Brain Res 2002;130:65–71.

Spencer TJ, Biederman J, Madras BK et al. In vivo neuroreceptor imaging in attention deficit/hyperactivity disorder: a focus on the dopamine transporter. Biol Psychiatry 2005;57:1293–300.

Spencer TJ, Faraone SV, Michelson D et al. Atomoxetine and adult attention deficit/hyperactivity disorder: the effects of comorbidity. J Clin Psychiatry 2006;67(3):415–20.

Stahl SM. Stahl's Essential Psychopharamcology, 3rd Edition, Cambridge University Press N.Y., 2008 (Chapter 17)

Steere JC and Arnsten AFT. The alpha 2A noradrenergic receptor agonist guanfacine improves visual object discrimination reversal performance in aged rhesus monkeys. Behav Neurosci 1997;111(5):883–91.

Surman CGH, Thomas RJ, Aleardi M et al. Adults with ADHD and sleep complaints. J Atten Disord 2006;9(3):550–5.

Swanson JM, Greenhill LL, Lopez FA et al. Modafinil film coated tablets in children and adolescents with attention deficit/hyperactivity disorder: results of a randomized, double-blind, placebo-controlled fixed dose study followed by abrupt discontinuation. J Clin Psychiatry 2006;67:137–47.

Tamm L, Menn V and Reiss AL. Parietal attentional system aberrations during target detection in adolescents with attention deficit hyperactivity disorder: event-related fMRI evidence. Am J Psychiatry 2006;163:1033–43.

Taylor FB and Russo J. Efficacy of modafinil compared to dextroamphetamine for the treatment of attention deficit hyperactivity disorder in adults. J Child Adolesc Psychopharmacol 2000;10(4):311–20.

Turner DC, Clark L, Dowson J et al. Modafinil improves cognition and response inhibition in adult attention deficit/hyperactivity disorder. Biol Psychiatry 2004;55:1031–40.

Turner DC, Robbins TW, Clark L et al. Cognitive enhancing effects of modafinil in healthy volunteers. Psychopharmacology 2003;165:260–9.

Vaidya CJ, Bunge SA, Dudukovic NM et al. Altered neural substrates of cognitive control in childhood ADHD: evidence from functional magnetic resonance imaging. Am J Psychiatry 2005;162:1605–13.

Valera EM, Faraone SV, Biederman J et al. Functional neuroanatomy of working memory in adults with attention deficit/hyperactivity disorder. Biol Psychiatry 2005;57:439–47.

Volkow ND, Wang GJ, Newcorn J et al. Depressed dopamine activity in caudate and preliminary evidence of limbic involvement in adults with attention deficit/hyperactivity disorder. Arch Gen Psychiatry 2007;64(8):932–40.

Weiss M, Safren SA, Solanto MV et al. Research forum on psychological treatment of adults with ADHD. J Atten Disord 2008;11:642-51.

Wilens TE and Dodson W. A clinical perspective of attention deficit/hyperactivity disorder into adulthood. J Clin Psychiatry 2004;65(10):1301–13.

Wilens TE. Lisdexamfetamine for ADHD. Curr Psychiatry 2007;6:96–98, 105.

Wilson MC, Wilman AH, Bell EC et al. Dextroamphetamine causes a change in regional brain activity in vivo during cognitive tasks: a functional magnetic resonance imaging study of blood oxygen level dependent response. Biol Psychiatry 2004;56:284–91.

Zang YF, Jin Z, Weng XC et al. Functional MRI in attention deficit hyperactivity disorder: evidence for hypofrontality. Brain Dev 2005;27:544–50.

Zuvekas SH, Vitiello B and Norquist GS. Recent trends in stimulant medication use among US children. Am J Psychiatry 2006;163:579–85.

Appendix: Rating Scales

ADHD Rating Scale

Child's Name:

Age:

Filled Out By:

Child's Sex: ___M ___F

Date:

DIRECTIONS:
Below is a list of items that describes pupils. For each item that describes the pupil, now or within the past week, check whether the item is *Not True, Somewhat or Sometimes True, or Very or Often True*. Please check all items as well as you can, even if some do not seem to apply to this pupil.

		Not True	Somewhat or Sometimes True	Very or Often True
1.	Fails to finish things he/she starts	[ ]	[ ]	[ ]
2.	Can't concentrate, can't pay attention for long	[ ]	[ ]	[ ]
3.	Can't sit still, restless, or hyperactive	[ ]	[ ]	[ ]
4.	Fidgets	[ ]	[ ]	[ ]
5.	Daydreams or gets lost in his/her thoughts	[ ]	[ ]	[ ]
6.	Impulsive or acts without thinking	[ ]	[ ]	[ ]
7.	Difficulty following directions	[ ]	[ ]	[ ]
8.	Talks out of turn	[ ]	[ ]	[ ]
9.	Messy work	[ ]	[ ]	[ ]
10.	Inattentive, easily distracted	[ ]	[ ]	[ ]
11.	Talks too much	[ ]	[ ]	[ ]
12.	Fails to carry out assigned tasks	[ ]	[ ]	[ ]

Please feel free to write any comments about the pupil's work or behavior in the last week:

Wender Utah Rating Scale

Questions Associated with ADHD

- 25 of the 61 questions were associated with ADHD as follows; 5 possible responses scored from 0-4 pts; not at all or very slightly=0, mildly, moderately=2, quite a bit=3, very much=4.

As a child I was (or had):	
3.	concentration problems, easily distracted
4.	anxious worrying
5.	nervous fidgety
6.	inattentive daydreaming
7.	hot- or short-tempered, low boiling point
9.	temper outbursts, tantrums
10.	trouble with stick-to-it-tiveness, not following through, failing to finish things started
11.	stubborn, strong-willed
12.	sad or blue, depressed, unhappy
15.	disobedient with parents, rebellious, sassy
16.	low opinions of myself
17.	irritable
20.	moody, ups and downs
21.	angry
24.	acting without thinking, impulsive
25.	tendency to be immature
26.	guilty feelings, regretful
27.	losing control of myself
28.	tendency to be or act irrational
29.	unpopular with other children, didn't keep friends for long, didn't get along with other children
40.	trouble seeing things from someone else's point of view
41.	trouble with authorities, trouble with school, visits to principal's office
As a child in school I was (or had):	
51.	overall a poor student, slow learner
56.	trouble with mathematics or numbers
59.	not achieving up to potential

Wender Utah rating scale subscore=_____ (sum of 25 questions associated with ADHD)

Interpretation:

- minimum score for the 25 questions is 0
- maximum score 100
- if a cutoff score of 46 was used 86% of patients with ADHD, 99% of normal persons and 81% of depressed subjects were correctly classified

Snap-IV Rating Scale

The SNAP-IV Teacher and Parent Rating Scale

James M. Swanson, Ph.D., University of California, Irvine, CA 92715

Name:_____

Gender:_____ Age:_____ Grade:_____

Ethnicity (circle one which best applies):

African-American   Asian   Caucasian   Hispanic

Completed by:_____

Type of Class:_____ Class size:_____

For each item, check the column which best describes this child:

Not at all, Just A Little, Quite A Bit, Very Much

		Not at All	Just a Little	Quite a Bit	Very Much
1.	Often fails to give close attention to details or makes careless mistakes in schoolwork or tasks				
2.	Often has difficulty sustaining attention in tasks or play activities				
3.	Often does not seem to listen when spoken to directly				
4.	Often does not follow through on instructions and fails to finish schoolwork, chores, or duties				
5.	Often has difficulty organizing tasks and activities				
6.	Often avoids, dislikes, or reluctantly engages in tasks requiring sustained mental effort				
7.	Often loses things necessary for activities (e.g., toys, school assignments, pencils, or books)				
8.	Often is distracted by extraneous stimuli				
9.	Often is forgetful in daily activities				
10.	Often has difficulty maintaining alertness, orienting to requests, or executing directions				
11.	Often fidgets with hands or feet or squirms in seat				
12.	Often leaves seat in classroom or in other situations in which remaining seated is expected				
13.	Often runs about or climbs excessively in situations in which it is inappropriate				
14.	Often has difficulty playing or engaging in leisure activities quietly				
15.	Often is "on the go" or often acts as if "driven by a motor"				
16.	Often talks excessively				

Snap-IV Rating Scale (cont'd)

For each item, check the column which best describes this child:

Not at all, Just A Little, Quite A Bit, Very Much

		Not at All	Just a Little	Quite a Bit	Very Much
17.	Often blurts out answers before questions have been completed				
18.	Often has difficulty awaiting turn				
19.	Often interrupts or intrudes on others (e.g., butts into conversations/games)				
20.	Often has difficulty sitting still, being quiet, or inhibiting impulses in the classroom or at home				
21.	Often loses temper				
22.	Often argues with adults				
23.	Often actively defies or refuses adult requests or rules				
24.	Often deliberately does things that annoy other people				
25.	Often blames others for his or her mistakes or misbehavior				
26.	Often touchy or easily annoyed by others				
27.	Often is angry and resentful				
28.	Often is spiteful or vindictive				
29.	Often is quarrelsome				
30.	Often is negative, defiant, disobedient, or hostile toward authority figures				
31.	Often makes noises (e.g., humming or odd sounds)				
32.	Often is excitable, impulsive				
33.	Often cries easily				
34.	Often is uncooperative				
35.	Often acts "smart"				
36.	Often is restless or overactive				
37.	Often disturbs other children				
38.	Often changes mood quickly and drastically				
39.	Often easily frustrated if demand are not met immediately				
40.	Often teases other children and interferes with their activities				
41.	Often is aggressive to other children (e.g., picks fights or bullies)				
42.	Often is destructive with property of others (e.g., vandalism)				
43.	Often is deceitful (e.g., steals, lies, forges, copies the work of others, or "cons" others)				

Snap-IV Rating Scale (cont'd)

For each item, check the column which best describes this child:

Not at all, Just A Little, Quite A Bit, Very Much

		Not at All	Just a Little	Quite a Bit	Very Much
44.	Often and seriously violates rules (e.g., is truant, runs away, or completely ignores class rules)				
45.	Has persistent pattern of violating the basic rights of others or major societal norms				
46.	Has episodes of failure to resist aggressive impulses (to assault others or to destroy property)				
47.	Has motor or verbal tics (sudden, rapid, recurrent, nonrhythmic motor or verbal activity)				
48.	Has repetitive motor behavior (e.g., hand waving, body rocking, or picking at skin)				
49.	Has obsessions (persistent and intrusive inappropriate ideas, thoughts, or impulses)				
50.	Has compulsions (repetitive behaviors or mental acts to reduce anxiety or distress)				
51.	Often is restless or seems keyed up or on edge				
52.	Often is easily fatigued				
53.	Often has difficulty concentrating (mind goes blank)				
54.	Often is irritable				
55.	Often has muscle tension				
56.	Often has excessive anxiety and worry (e.g., apprehensive expectation)				
57.	Often has daytime sleepiness (unintended sleeping in inappropriate situations)				
58.	Often has excessive emotionality and attention-seeking behavior				
59.	Often has need for undue admiration, grandiose behavior, or lack of empathy				
60.	Often has instability in relationships with others, reactive mood, and impulsivity				
61.	Sometimes for at least a week has inflated self esteem or grandiosity				
62.	Sometimes for at least a week is more talkative than usual or seems pressured to keep talking				
63.	Sometimes for at least a week has flight of ideas or says that thoughts are racing				

Snap-IV Rating Scale (cont'd)

For each item, check the column which best describes this child:

Not at all, Just A Little, Quite A Bit, Very Much

		Not at All	Just a Little	Quite a Bit	Very Much
64.	Sometimes for at least a week has elevated, expansive or euphoric mood				
65.	Sometimes for at least a week is excessively involved in pleasurable but risky activities				
66.	Sometimes for at least 2 weeks has depressed mood (sad, hopeless, discouraged)				
67.	Sometimes for at least 2 weeks has irritable or cranky mood (not just when frustrated)				
68.	Sometimes for at least 2 weeks has markedly diminished interest or pleasure in most activities				
69.	Sometimes for at least 2 weeks has psychomotor agitation (even more active than usual)				
70.	Sometimes for at least 2 weeks has psychomotor retardation (slowed down in most activities)				
71.	Sometimes for at least 2 weeks is fatigued or has loss of energy				
72.	Sometimes for at least 2 weeks has feelings of worthlessness or excessive, inappropriate guilt				
73.	Sometimes for at least 2 weeks has diminished ability to think or concentrate				
74.	Chronic low self-esteem most of the time for at least a year				
75.	Chronic poor concentration or difficulty making decisions most of the time for at least a year				
76.	Chronic feelings of hopelessness most of the time for at least a year				
77.	Currently is hypervigilant (overly watchful or alert) or has exaggerated startle response				
78.	Currently is irritable, has anger outbursts, or has difficulty concentrating				
79.	Currently has an emotional (e.g., nervous, worried, hopeless, tearful) response to stress				
80.	Currently has a behavioral (e.g., fighting, vandalism, truancy) response to stress				
81.	Has difficulty getting started on classroom assignments				
82.	Has difficulty staying on task for an entire classroom period				
83.	Has problems in completion of work on classroom assignments				

Snap-IV Rating Scale (cont'd)

For each item, check the column which best describes this child:

Not at all, Just A Little, Quite A Bit, Very Much

		Not at All	Just a Little	Quite a Bit	Very Much
84.	Has problems in accuracy or neatness of written work in the classroom				
85.	Has difficulty attending to a group classroom activity or discussion				
86.	Has difficulty making transitions to the next topic or classroom period				
87.	Has problems in interactions with peers in the classroom				
88.	Has problems in interactions with staff (teacher or aide)				
89.	Has difficulty remaining quiet according to classroom rules				
90.	Has difficulty staying seated according to classroom rules				

The SWAN* Rating Scale for ADHD

Child's name:_____ Gender:_____ Age: _____

Completed by:_____ (circle one) Parent Teacher Physician

Date Completed:_____

For each item, check the column that best describes this child over the past six months.

		Not at all	Just a Little	Quite a bit	Very much
1.	Gives close attention to detail and avoids careless mistakes	____	____	____	____
2.	Sustains attention on tasks or play activities	____	____	____	____
3.	Listens when spoken to directly	____	____	____	____
4.	Follows through on instructions; finishes school work and chores	____	____	____	____
5.	Organizes tasks and activities	____	____	____	____
6.	Engages in tasks that require sustained mental effort	____	____	____	____
7.	Keeps track of things necessary for activities (doesn't lose them)	____	____	____	____
8.	Ignores extraneous stimuli	____	____	____	____
9.	Remembers daily activities	____	____	____	____
10.	Sits still (controls movement of hands or feet or controls squirming)	____	____	____	____
11.	Stays seated (when required by class rules or social conventions)	____	____	____	____
12.	Modulates motor activity (inhibits inappropriate running or climbing)	____	____	____	____
13.	Plays quietly (keeps noise level reasonable)	____	____	____	____
14.	Settles down and rests (controls constant activity)	____	____	____	____
15.	Modulates verbal activity (controls excessive talking)	____	____	____	____
16.	Reflects on questions (controls blurting out answers)	____	____	____	____
17.	Awaits turn (stands in line and takes turns)	____	____	____	____
18.	Enters into conversation and games without interrupting or intruding	____	____	____	____

The SWAN* Rating Scale for ADHD (cont'd)

Scoring Section: For each question, place a 1 next to the question number below if the response was "not at all" or "just a little" and a 0 if the response was "quite a bit" or "very much".

1. ____		10. ____	
2. ____		11. ____	
3. ____		12. ____	
4. ____		13. ____	
5. ____		14. ____	
6. ____		15. ____	
7. ____		16. ____	
8. ____		17. ____	
9. ____		18. ____	

Sum #'s 1-9 ____   **Sum #'s 10-18** ____

*Adapted from James M. Swanson, Ph.D., University of California, Irvine

Results:

1. If the sum of 1-9 is 6 or greater, the child is likely ADHD- Inattentive type. Consider mental health evaluation.

2. If the sum of 10-18 is 6 or greater, the child is likely ADHD Hyperactive/Impulsive type. Consider mental health evaluation.

3. If both the sums of 1-9 and 10-18 are 6 or greater, the child is likely ADHD-Combined type. Consider mental health evaluation.

4. If neither sums are 6 or greater, the child likely does not have ADHD or the symptoms are being controlled with current treatment.

Adults ADHD Self-Report Scale (ASRS-v1.1) Symptom Checklist

Patient Name						Today's Date		

Please answer the questions below, rating yourself on each of the criteria shown using the scale on the right side of the page. As you answer each question, place an X in the box that best describes how you have felt and conducted yourself over the past 6 months. Please give this completed checklist to your healthcare professional to discuss during today's appointment.	Never	Rarely	Sometimes	Often	Very Often
1. How often do you have trouble wrapping up the final details of a project, once the challenging parts have been done?					
2. How often do you have difficulty getting things in order when you have to do a task that requires organization?					
3. How often do you have problems remembering appointments or obligations?					
4. When you have a task that requires a lot of thought, how often do you avoid or delay getting started?					
5. How often do you fidget or squirm with your hands or feet when you have to sit down for a long time?					
6. How often do you feel overly active and compelled to do things, like you were driven by a motor?					

Part A

	Never	Rarely	Sometimes	Often	Very Often
7. How often do you make careless mistakes when you have to work on a boring or difficult project?					
8. How often do you have difficulty keeping your attention when you are doing boring or repetitive work?					
9. How often do you have difficulty concentrating on what people say to you, even when they are speaking to you directly?					
10. How often do you have misplace or have difficulty finding things at home or at work?					
11. How often are you distracted by activity or noise around you?					
12. How often do you leave your seat in meetings or other situations in which you are expected to remain seated?					
13. How often do you feel restless or fidgety?					
14. How often do you have difficulty unwinding and relaxing when you have time to yourself?					
15. How often do you find yourself talking too much when you are in social situations?					
16. When you're in a conversation, how often do you find yourself finishing the sentences of the people you are talking to, before they can finish themselves?					
17. How often do you have difficulty waiting your turn in situations when turn taking is required?					
18. How often do you interrupt others when they are busy?					

Part B

Everything You Wanted to Know About ADHD But Forgot You Wanted to Ask

CME Posttest

To receive your certificate of CME credit or participation, please complete the posttest (you must score at least 70% to receive credit) and activity evaluation answer sheet found on the last page and return it by mail or fax it to 760-931-8713. Once received, your posttest will be graded and, along with your certificate (if a score of 70% or more was attained), returned to you by mail. Alternatively, you may complete these items online and immediately print your certificate at **www.neiglobal.com/cme**. There is no fee for this activity. **Please circle the correct answer on the answer sheet provided.**

1. Brian, a 35-year-old attorney and father of two, complains of having been advised by his supervisor to seek medical attention as he often misplaces his keys, misses his appointments, has a tendency to interrupt people during meetings, and appears to party excessively on weeknights. Brian asserts that he has a lot of projects on his mind, merely stands up for himself in meetings, and just tries to relax in the evening. Recognizing possible ADHD, what might be the best way to start your questions when interviewing this adult?

    A. Compared to your parents, how often do you…
    B. Compared to other people your age, how often do you …
    C. Compared to your childhood, how often do you …
    D. Compared to your children, how often do you …

2. You are a clinician in a very busy practice and are giving different screening questionnaires to your patients to fill out as they are waiting for their appointment. Which rating scale has a screener that can be used to discern adult ADHD?

    A. Connor's ADHD Rating Scale for Adults
    B. Wender Utah Rating Scale
    C. Brown ADD Scale for Adults
    D. Adult ADHD Rating Scale

3. Compared to their effects in children, properly-dosed stimulants in adults are:

    A. as effective as in children
    B. less effective as in children
    C. more effective as in children

4. Isabelle, a 25-year-old saleswoman, recently got promoted to sales manager and oversees three other sales reps. Although she used to excel in the fast-paced world of sales, she has now hit a roadblock and becomes very disorganized every time she needs to consolidate her department sales and write up her monthly report. She gets especially incapacitated when she has to troubleshoot inaccuracies in the books. Recently her appearance is lacking as well, and she has lost three company phones in the last month. What brain area is theoretically most likely to be impaired in this woman?

    A. Dorsolateral Prefrontal Cortex
    B. Prefrontal Motor Cortex
    C. Orbital Frontal Cortex
    D. Supplementary Motor Cortex

5. A 6-year-old child has frequently been asked by the teacher to remain seated during class, and to pay attention. These symptoms can be bothersome to the class, but the tendency of the child to blurt out her thoughts and yell out answers is most distracting. To explain impulsive blurting out, which loop is theoretically most likely out of tune in this child?

    A. DLPFC to striatum to thalamus to DLPFC
    B. Dorsal ACC to bottom of striatum to thalamus to ACC
    C. Subgenual ACC to nucleus accumbens to thalamus to cortex
    D. OFC to bottom of striatum to thalamus to OFC
    E. Prefrontal motor cortex to lateral striatum to thalamus to cortex

6. Alex was diagnosed with ADHD when he was 6. While he used to properly take his medication as a child and young adolescent, he has been reluctant to continue his treatment since the age of 16. He has been primarily self-medicating with alcohol and cigarettes for a while. Now 25 and employed as a bartender, he seeks medical help again, as he feels a bit overwhelmed with his new job and other responsibilities. You decide to put him on 80 mg/day of atomoxetine (Strattera), one of the non-stimulant medications effective in ADHD. Why does atomoxetine lack abuse potential?

   A. It decreases norepinephrine levels in the nucleus accumbens, but not in the prefrontal cortex.
   B. It increases dopamine levels in the prefrontal cortex but not in the nucleus accumbens.
   C. It modulates serotonin levels in the raphe nucleus.
   D. It increases dopamine in the striatum and anterior cingulate cortex.

7. Samuel, a creative 15-year-old with ADHD, has a hard time in his math class. When the teacher asks him to stay focused on one task, to organize his work, and to follow through with the task at hand, he often fails. Problem solving, though, is probably his worst enemy. His pediatrician suggests testing his sustained attention using the _____ to see if the_____ is aberrantly activated on an fMRI.

   A. Stroop task; orbital frontal cortex
   C. Stroop task; anterior cingulate cortex
   B. N-back test; prefrontal motor cortex
   D. N-back test; dorsolateral prefrontal cortex

8. As chief resident, you are attending a CME lecture on attention-deficit/hyperactivity disorder in order to brush up for the boards. Your PGY II colleague in the audience, asks the lecturer: "What is the difference between syndromatic and symptomatic persistence?" Which is the answer given by the lecturer?

   A. Symptomatic persistence is the loss of partial diagnostic status without functional recovery.
   B. Syndromatic persistence is the loss of partial diagnostic status without functional recovery.
   C. Symptomatic persistence refers to functional recovery.
   D. Syndromatic persistence refers to functional recovery.

9. In a world where acronyms are key, you want to make sure that everyone in your practice is talking about the same thing when you use those acronyms. You are posting a list of acronyms. Which one is correct?

   A. DLPFC – deep layer parietal frontal cortex
   C. OFC – olfactory cortex
   B. CSTC – cortical striatal thalamo-cortical
   D. ACC – anterior corpus callosum

10. Your neuroscience teacher has just flown through the difference between methylphenidate and amphetamine, and phasic versus tonic stimulation leading to abuse. As you did not catch everything, you are collecting your friends' notes. Although your friends' versions explain the difference between methylphenidate and amphetamine similarly, they all differ on the explanation between pulsatile versus tonic stimulation. Which version is correct?

   A. Pulsatile stimulation amplifies undesirable phasic DA and NE firing, which can lead to euphoria and abuse.
   B. Immediate-release stimulants lead to tonic firing, which can lead to euphoria and abuse.
   C. Tonic firing is the result of rapid receptor occupancy and fast onset of action, as seen with extended-release formulations.
   D. Extended-release stimulants result in phasic stimulation of NE and DA signals, but this does not lead to euphoria and abuse.

Everything You Wanted to Know About ADHD...But Forgot You Wanted to Ask

Posttest and Activity Evaluation Answer Sheet

Please complete the posttest and activity evaluation answer sheet on this page and return by mail or fax. Alternatively, <u>you may complete these items online and immediately print your certificate</u> at **www.neiglobal.com/cme.** (Please circle the correct answers)

Posttest Answer Sheet (score of 70% or higher required for CME credit)

1.	A B C D	**6.**	A B C D
2.	A B C D	**7.**	A B C D
3.	A B C	**8.**	A B C D
4.	A B C D	**9.**	A B C D
5.	A B C D E	**10.**	A B C D

Activity Evaluation: Please rate the following, using a scale of:

1-poor   2-below average   3-average   4-above average   5-excellent

1. The overall quality of the content was…   1 2 3 4 5

2. The relevance of the content to my professional needs was…   1 2 3 4 5

3. The level at which the learning objective was met of teaching me to recognize   1 2 3 4 5
    how ADHD symptoms change as a patient grows up and how previously unrec-
    ognized ADHD can manifest in an adult

4. The level at which the learning objective was met of teaching me to use mea-   1 2 3 4 5
    surement tools to track a patient's symptoms

5. The level at which the learning objective was met of teaching me to better assess   1 2 3 4 5
    comorbid illness in adult ADHD patients in order to maximize treatment

6. The level at which the learning objective was met of teaching me to integrate   1 2 3 4 5
    new treatment formulations and therapy into current practice

7. The level at which this activity was objective, scientifically balanced, and free of   1 2 3 4 5
    commercial bias was…

8. The overall quality of this activity was…   1 2 3 4 5

9. Based on my experience and knowledge, the level of this activity was:

    Too Basic   Basic   Appropriate   Complex   Too Complex

Continued on back

10. Based on the information presented in this activity, I will:

    A. Change my practice.
    B. Seek additional information on this topic.
    C. Do nothing as current practice reflects activity's recommendations
    D. Do nothing as the content was not convincing

11. What barriers might keep you from implementing changes in your practice you'd like to make as a result of participating in this activity?

12. The following additional information about this topic would help me in my practice:

13. How could this activity have been improved?

14. Additional comments:

Name: _____ Credentials: _____

Address: _____

_____

City, State, Zip: _____

Email: _____

Phone: _____ Fax: _____

Mail or fax <u>both sides</u> of this form to:

CME Department   Fax: 760-931-8713
Neuroscience Education Institute
1930 Palomar Point Way, Suite 101
Carlsbad, CA 92008